Country and City Detective

UNITS 42, 43 STORYBOOK

ISBN 1-59318-508-1

10 09 08 07 06 05   1 2 3 4 5 6

SOPRIS WEST™ EDUCATIONAL SERVICES
A CAMBIUM LEARNING COMPANY

BOSTON, MA • LONGMONT, CO

UNIT 42 • Country Detective

Carlos the Curious

Planning Assistance: See Daily Lesson Planning for scheduling.

UNIT 43 • City Detective

Maya the Magnificent

Planning Assistance: See Daily Lesson Planning for scheduling.

Country Detective

By Marilyn Sprick
Illustrated by Selina Alko

UNIT 42 STORY

Carlos the Curious

Vocabulary Words

curious
Someone who is curious asks a lot of questions.

determine
Determine means to figure something out.

discouraged
Someone who is discouraged is unhappy and worried about something.

Try defining the next words. Then, look the words up in the glossary.

clue
Start with "A clue is . . ."

detective
Start with "A detective is someone who . . ."

Carlos the Curious

CHAPTER 1

Something Strange

I live in the country. I am eight years old. I like to play baseball and swim. I like to read books. My favorite book is *Nate the Great*. Nate is a detective. He is very curious. He asks many questions. I think that I too can be a detective. I like to ask questions and search for answers. My name is Carlos the Curious.

It was a Tuesday afternoon. I was walking home from school with my best friend, George, when I thought to myself, "Something is strange. Something is different. What is it?" George and I walked a few more blocks.

"That's it!" I said.

George looked surprised. "What's it?"

I said, "George, why are you wearing your helmet?"

Who is the story about? Carlos thinks it's strange for George to be wearing his bike helmet. Look at the picture. What's strange about George wearing a bike helmet?

George said, "I always wear my helmet on my way home from school."

I looked at George and said, "Yes, but you wear your helmet when you are riding your bike. Where is your bike?"

George looked discouraged and shrugged his shoulders.

Who is the main character? What do you know about Carlos? Who else is in the story? What do you know about George? Carlos thought something was different or strange. What was that? At the end of the chapter, George was discouraged. What does it mean to be discouraged? Read the next chapter to find out why George isn't riding his bike home.

CHAPTER 2

My First Case

Who is the story about? In the last chapter, George was discouraged. What do you think you will find out in this chapter?

George and I were walking home from school. George was wearing his bicycle helmet, but he had no bike. I had asked him, "Where is your new bike?" George had shrugged his shoulders. So I asked again, "Where is your bike?"

George said, "I left my bike at school."

George didn't say anything more. So I didn't either. We walked along the dusty path. I stopped to inspect a termite nest, an anthill, and a rotten old log. George walked slowly—still wearing his helmet.

The sun was shining. George was looking very hot. Finally I said, "George, why did you leave your bike at school?"

George said, "I can't unlock it." George didn't say anything more, so I didn't either. We walked farther down the dusty path. I stopped to inspect under a rock. A snake had shed its skin.

When we were near our homes, I asked, "Is your bicycle key lost?"

George said, "Yup."

I said, "This is great! My first case—The Case of the Missing Key! I think that I would make a great detective. Do you want me to help you find your key?"

George said, "Yup."

What was George's problem? What is Carlos going to help George do? Carlos said, "This is great!" Carlos seems excited. Why is he excited about the lost key?

CHAPTER 3

The Case of the Missing Key

Who is the main character? What do you know about him? Who else is in the story? What is George's problem?

George had lost the key to his bicycle lock, so he was walking home with me. George agreed to let me help him find his key. Wow! I had my first real case—The Case of the Missing Key.

I went home first. Mom had left me a note.

Carlos,

I've gone to the store. I will be back at 4:00.

Love,
Mama

I left Mom a note. I always leave her a note when I go somewhere.

Mama,

I'm at George's house. I will be back at 4:30.

Love,
Carlos

I went across the path to George's house. He still had his helmet on. We each ate an apple. Food helps me think. I said, "I'm curious. Where did you have your key last?"

George said, "If I remembered that, my key would not be missing." George looked discouraged.

Carlos left his mother a note. What did it say? Why do you think Carlos left his mother a note? George looked discouraged. What does that mean?

I said, "You are right. Let me ask you some more questions." Then I dug in my backpack. I took out a notepad. A detective always takes notes so he doesn't miss a clue.

I asked, "Where is your bike?"

George frowned and said, "At school."

I nodded. I wrote "The Case of the Missing Key" at the top of the notepad. Then I wrote "Clues." Under "Clues," I wrote "1. Bike at school."

Who is the story about? What do you know about Carlos? What do you know about George? What has Carlos learned about the missing key? Read the next chapter. You will learn new clues. Perhaps you can figure out where the missing key is.

CHAPTER 4

More Questions

George had lost the key to his bike. I, Carlos the Curious, had offered to help him find his key. I had determined that the bike was at school.

Next I asked, "Is the bike locked?"

George frowned again and nodded.

I wrote "2. Bike locked."

I said, "This is great. I have learned that your bike is at school, and it is locked. So, you must have had your key this morning. Where do you keep your key?"

George said, "In my pocket."

I wrote in my notepad "3. Keeps key in his pocket."

I asked, "Can you show me your pocket?"

George reached down and turned his pocket inside out. There was a big hole in his pocket. I wrote "4. Big hole in pocket."

What was clue number four? What do you think happened to George's key?

CHAPTER 5

The Clues

Who is the story about? Tell something about each character. What do the boys want? What clues have they found?

I said to George, "I think we are on the right track. We have many clues. Look at my notes." George began to read my notes.

I explained, "The clues tell us we must go back to school. Once we are there, we will leave no stone unturned. We will inspect every inch of the path from the bike rack to the school. I, Carlos the Curious, have almost solved the case."

The Case of the Missing Key

Clues
1. Bike at school
2. Bike locked
3. Keeps key in his pocket
4. Big hole in pocket

George and I asked George's mother, Mrs. Martinez, if we could go back to school. We always ask if it is okay to go somewhere. Mrs. Martinez said, "Yes, and good luck with the case. George is very attached to his bike, and I think he would not look so funny wearing a helmet if he had his bike."

What is missing? After reading the clues, where does Carlos think the key will be found? Read the next chapter to see if Carlos has solved the mystery.

CHAPTER 6

Discouraged

Who is the story about? Tell something about each character. What do the boys want? What clues have they found? Read the chapter title again. Do you think the boys will find the missing key?

I had a lot of clues about the missing key. I had determined that George and I needed to inspect around and near George's bike. We walked quickly back to school. This time I did not stop to inspect the termite nest, the anthill, or the rotten log. I had a job to do.

Back at school, I looked at my notes. I said, "George, show me your bike." George looked at me and looked at his new bike. It was still locked in the bike rack. I jiggled the lock. It was locked. I took out my notepad and wrote, "5. Bicycle lock is locked." Then I said, "We must inspect all around the bike rack."

George and I inspected all around the bike rack and on the path to the school door. There was a candy wrapper and a quarter but no key. We threw the candy wrapper in the trash can, and we decided to take the quarter to the principal in the morning.

I added more notes to my notepad.

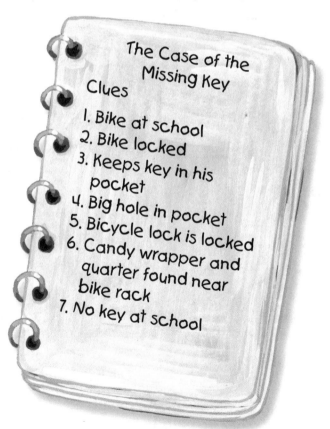

The Case of the Missing Key

Clues

1. Bike at school
2. Bike locked
3. Keeps key in his pocket
4. Big hole in pocket
5. Bicycle lock is locked
6. Candy wrapper and quarter found near bike rack
7. No key at school

I looked at my watch. It was 4:10. I had told my mother I would be back by 4:30. It was time to go. George looked discouraged.

How does George look? Why is he discouraged?

CHAPTER 7

Case Solved

What do the boys want? Why was George discouraged at the end of the last chapter?

George and I had not found George's key at school. I had asked all the right questions, but we didn't have the right answer. At school, we had left no stone unturned.

We walked back home. George was still wearing his helmet. He kicked at the stones on the dusty path. Then he began walking slower and limping. I asked, "George, why are you limping?" George sat down on the side of the path. I said, "I will be late. Mama will worry." He pulled off his shoe and shook it.

Something fell out and went "plop."

"That's it! It's your key," I yelled. George smiled and ran back to school to get his bike.

What just happened? Where had the key been?

Back at home, George locked his bike to the mailbox. Then he put his key in his shirt pocket. Finally, he took his helmet off and hung it on his bike. We went to my house. We each had a big glass of milk.

We told Mama all about The Case of the Missing Key. Mama gave George a big key ring. George put his key on it and clipped it to his belt loop.

Was the case solved? How do you think the boys felt?

I wrote in my notepad, "Key found in shoe. Case closed."

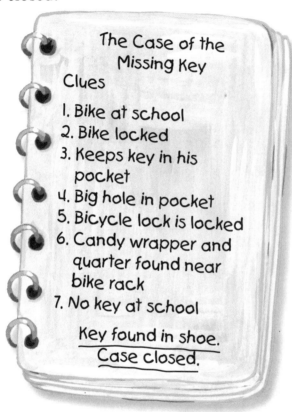

The Case of the Missing Key

Clues

1. Bike at school
2. Bike locked
3. Keeps key in his pocket
4. Big hole in pocket
5. Bicycle lock is locked
6. Candy wrapper and quarter found near bike rack
7. No key at school

Key found in shoe.
Case closed.

CARLOS THE CURIOUS COUNTRY DETECTIVE

CARLOS THE CURIOUS

We're going to retell the story.
What was the title of the story?
Who was the main character?
Who else was in the story?
Describe each of the characters.

● Beginning—Problem
Who had the problem at the beginning of the story? How did Carlos know there was a problem?

■ Middle—Goal, Action
What were Carlos and George trying to do?
What did they do to find the missing key?

▲ Ending
What happened at the end?

Unit 42 Glossary

clue

> A clue is something that helps us find something.

curious

> Someone who is curious asks a lot of questions.

detective

> A detective is someone who finds missing things. A detective solves problems.

determine

> Determine means to <u>figure</u> something out.

discouraged

> Someone who is discouraged is unhappy and worried about something.

Storybook Decoding Review

Words with and without the Bossy E:

home	page	bike	wrote
not	note	takes	hole
skate	stone	car	care

Words you can sound out:

page	dusty	farther	George
frown	explain	threw	shirt
walking	school	unlock	strange

Words you have learned:

answer	country	thought	either
enough	most	curious	change

Phrases you can read:

Where there's a will there's a way.

Two heads are better then one.

Sentences you can read:

At the beginning of the story, George lost his bike key.

In the middle of the story, Carlos made a list of clues and looked for the key.

At the end of the story, Carlos and George found the bike key.

City Detective

By Marilyn Sprick
Illustrated by Cindy Revell

Maya the
Magnificent
City
Detective

UNIT 43 STORY

Maya the Magnificent

Vocabulary Words

city
A city is a place where many people live and work. A city has many buildings and streets.

inspect
Inspect means to look carefully at something.

magnificent
Something that is great is magnificent. Another word for "great" is "magnificent."

pearl
A pearl is a white jewel that has grown inside an oyster. A string of pearls is a necklace made of pearls.

Try defining the next word. Then, look the word up in the glossary.

apartment
Start with "An apartment is a place . . ."

Maya the Magnificent

CHAPTER 1

The Lost Pearls

I live in the city. I am nine years old. I wear beads in my hair. I like to sing. I have a big smile, and people say I have pearly white teeth. My favorite book is *Nate the Great*. Nate is a detective. I have decided that I too can be a detective. My name is Maya the Magnificent.

It was a Monday afternoon. I had just gotten home from school when there was a tap at the door. It was old Mrs. Jefferson from Apartment 8A. We call her Mrs. J.

Mrs. J usually has a big smile for me. Today, there was no smile. Her mouth looked puckered and sad. Mrs. J got right down to business. She said, "Your door says, 'Maya the Magnificent, City Detective.' Do you find things?"

I nodded.

Mrs. J asked, "What is your fee?"

I said, "If I find what you are looking for, my fee is one dollar."

Mrs. J said, "I have lost my pearls. If you find them, I will pay you five dollars!"

Who is the main character? What do you know about Maya? What is Mrs. J's problem? What are pearls? Read the next chapter to find out whether Maya takes the job.

CHAPTER 2
Bruce

I thought of Mrs. J in her Sunday best. She always wore her red dress, a red hat, and a string of big white pearls. Mrs. J was willing to pay me five dollars to find her lost pearls.

I said, "Do not fear. I, Maya the Magnificent, will help you find your pearls."

Mrs. J nodded, but she did not smile. I said, "We have work to do. Where did you have the pearls last?"

Mrs. J said, "I do not remember. If I remembered where I had them last, I would have them now."

I said, "You are right. I will get Bruce." (Bruce is my little brother. He is six. He goes where I go.) "We might find the pearls in your apartment. We will come look for clues."

What is the problem? Who will help Mrs. J find her pearls?

CHAPTER 3

The New Case

What is the story about? Who is the main character? What do you know about Maya? Who else is in the story? What is Mrs. J's problem?

My little brother, Bruce, was watching TV. I, Maya the Magnificent, had a new case. I had been hired to find Mrs. J's string of pearls. I couldn't leave Bruce alone, so I said, "Bruce, I have a case. We need to go down the hall to Mrs. J's."

Bruce thought about that, but he didn't move.

So I said, "You can be my assistant."

Bruce thought about that too, but he still didn't move.

So I said, "If we find the pearls, I will give you fifty cents." Bruce got up and came with me.

We went down the hall to Mrs. J's apartment. "Wa, waaaa . . . " We could hear Mr. Miller in Apartment 8D practicing his trombone. "Wa, waaa."

Mrs. J's door was open. She was waiting for us. Mrs. J sat in her rocking chair. She had a frown on her face, and her mouth still looked puckered and sad. She said, "Come in. Come in."

I inspected Mrs. J's small apartment. Nothing seemed out of place.

I said, "Mrs. J, everything looks pretty good here. It doesn't look like you've been robbed."

What did Maya inspect? What does "inspect" mean? Read the next chapter to find out what happened to the pearls. Are there any clues to follow?

CHAPTER 4

No Smile

I, Maya the Magnificent, was on a case with my assistant, Bruce. Old Mrs. J had lost her pearls.

Mrs. J said, "Without my pearls, I have no smile for the delivery boy. I have no smile for the mailman. I have no smile for the preacher. Come Sunday, if I don't have my pearls back, I can't go to church." Then Mrs. J shook her head and looked discouraged.

Bruce and I got to work. We decided to start with the bedroom. We looked on the bed. We looked in the bed. We looked under the bed. We made a mess, so Bruce and I remade the bed. Then we sat on the bed. There were no pearls in the bed.

I noticed a gray velvet box on the dresser. It was tucked behind some books. I opened the box. Mrs. J's pearls were right on top. Bruce and I were excited. We had found the pearls!

We ran to the living room with the pearls, but Mrs. J didn't smile. She just muttered, "Not those pearls! I am missing my pearly whites!"

There was a tap at the door. It was Mom.

What was the problem? What did Maya and Bruce do to find the pearls? Were they successful?

CHAPTER 5

The Clue

What is the story about? Who is the main character? What do you know about Maya? Who else is in the story? What is Mrs. J's problem?

Bruce and I were on a case—the case of the missing pearls. We had found Mrs. J's string of pearls, but Mrs. J still insisted she was missing her pearly whites. I, Maya the Magnificent, was puzzled. It was a mystery. We had found the pearls, but the pearly whites were still missing!

Bruce and I always get home before Mom does. When Mom gets home, we make dinner together. Bruce can't have milk, so he makes juice. Bruce likes juice. While Bruce was mixing up the juice, I told Mom about my case.

Mom said, "What do you think happened to Mrs. J's pearls?"

Bruce said, "They're gone. Someone took 'em."

I said, "Mrs. J says her pearls have gone missing. We found a string of pearls, but Mrs. J said they weren't the right ones. Mrs. J said that she won't go to church without her pearls."

Mom said, "That's strange. I wouldn't have thought Mrs. J would be so vain."

I said, "She won't smile without her pearls. Her mouth even looks puckered and sad."

Mom said, "I think there's a clue in what you just told me. Maya, smile for me. What does Mrs. J tell you when you smile?"

It was then that I, Maya the Magnificent, had the answer. I whooped, "Mrs. J is missing her teeth!"

What was Mrs. J missing? What was the clue that helped Maya figure out what was missing? Read the next chapter to see if the mystery is solved.

CHAPTER 6

The Pink Box

Old Mrs. J wouldn't smile. She was missing her false teeth. That's why her mouth looked puckered and sad. I grabbed Bruce, and we ran up the stairs to Apartment 8A.

We tapped on Mrs. J's door. I said, "Mrs. J, we want to find your pearly whites."

Mrs. J nodded and said, "Come in."

Mrs. J gave each of us a cookie. I said, "Mrs. J, you had your teeth when we played checkers after school." Mrs. J nodded.

Bruce said, "I'm thirsty."

Mrs. J said, "Maya, please get Bruce some juice." I went to the refrigerator. The juice pitcher was in the back. I spotted it right away. There was a little pink box on top of the pitcher. I picked up the box and gave it to Mrs. J.

What do you think is in the pink box?

CHAPTER 7

Case Closed

Who is the main character? Who else is in the story? What was Mrs. J's problem? How was the case solved?

I gave Mrs. J the small pink box that I found in the refrigerator. Mrs. J covered her mouth and began laughing. She laughed all the way to the bathroom. When Mrs. J came back, she had the biggest smile I ever saw. She was wearing her pearly white false teeth.

We each had another cookie. Mrs. J explained, "I remember now. I was getting ready for bed. I had put my teeth in the pink box. I had the box in one hand, and I was putting the pitcher away. Then someone came to the door. I put the pitcher in the refrigerator. I must have put my pearly whites in the refrigerator right along with the juice."

Mrs. J gave us our fee of five dollars. I gave Mrs. J a hug. Mrs. J said, "You are great detectives! I will recommend you to anyone who is missing their teeth!"

That night, I brushed my teeth three times. Then I lay in bed. I could see snow falling in the flashing city lights. I could hear the wind howling. I snuggled into my blanket and thought, "I, Maya the Magnificent, City Detective, have solved another case." It had been a good day.

How did Maya's case end? Describe Maya. What was Maya's fee for finding Mrs. J's false teeth? How did everyone feel at the end of the story? Why do you think Maya brushed her teeth three times? Show me what your mouth would look like if you had no teeth.

MAYA THE MAGNIFICENT AND CARLOS THE CURIOUS

Maya the Magnificent	Carlos the Curious
Main Character	**Main Character**

Favorite Book: *Nate the Great*	Favorite Book: *Nate the Great*
Job: Detective	Job: Detective
Age: Nine	Age: Eight
Girl	Boy
Problem	**Problem**
Mrs. J was missing her pearls.	George was missing the key to his bike lock.

What's the same about the main characters? What's the same about the problems?

Maya the Magnificent *(continued)*	Carlos the Curious *(continued)*
Goal • To solve the problem Maya needed to find the missing pearls.	**Goal • To solve the problem** Carlos needed to find the missing key.
Action • Asked questions • Inspected the apartment • Talked it over with Mom	**Action** • Asked questions • Inspected at school • Wrote down clues
Conclusion Maya found the missing teeth in Mrs. J's refrigerator. Case closed.	**Conclusion** Carlos and George found the missing key in George's shoe. Case closed.

What's the same about the goals? In both stories, the main characters needed to . . . At the end of the stories or in the conclusions, both characters . . . What happened in each of the cases?

Unit 43 Glossary

apartment

An apartment is a place where people live. Many people live in an apartment building.

city

A city is a place where many people live and work. A city has many buildings and streets.

inspect

Inspect means to look carefully at something.

magnificent

Something that is great is magnificent. Another word for "great" is "magnificent."

pearl

A pearl is a white jewel that has grown inside an oyster. A string of pearls is a necklace made of pearls.

Storybook Decoding Review

Words with and without the Bossy E:

clue	car	care	juice
wore	gave	excite	place

Words you can sound out:

jewel	beads	paid	grown
pencil	inspect	dresser	found
grabbed	smells	saw	space

magnificent   detective   fantastic

Words you have learned:

change	enough	move	here
most	open	through	thought

Phrases you can read:

Two heads are better than one.

Where there's a will there's a way.

Sentences you can read:

At the beginning of the story, Mrs. J was missing her pearls.

In the middle of the story, Maya looked for Mrs. J's pearls.

At the end of the story, the detectives found Mrs. J's pearly white false teeth.